To John and Linda, with love and a rainbow of flowers. —M.S.

To my favorite biologist. —B.G.

With immense gratitude to Jessica Thrasher, Director of Education and Outreach for the Colorado Stormwater Center. Thank you for your expert guidance and all you do to educate the community on being stewards of our waterways.

For information about permission to reproduce selections from this book, write to Permissions, W. W. Norton & Company, Inc., 500 Fifth Avenue, New York, NY 10110

For information about special discounts for bulk purchases, please contact W. W. Norton Special Sales at specialsales@wwnorton.com or 800-233-4830

Manufacturing by RRD Asia
Book design by Hana Anouk Nakamura
Production manager: Delaney Adams

ISBN: 978-1-324-05235-7

W. W. Norton & Company, Inc.
500 Fifth Avenue, New York, N.Y. 10110
www.wwnorton.com

W. W. Norton & Company Ltd.
15 Carlisle Street, London W1D 3BS

1 2 3 4 5 6 7 8 9 0

Michelle Schaub

Illustrated by
Blanca Gómez

A Place
for Rain

Norton Young Readers
An Imprint of W. W. Norton & Company
Independent Publishers Since 1923

Plink.
Plip.
Plop.

We watch the raindrops drop.

Pitter-patter,
splutter-splatter,

drizzle turns to roar.

DOWNPOUR!

A rooftop-rushing,
gutter-gushing,
downspout-flushing
raindrop swarm.

SCHOOL

Look at all that water race,
swelling, sogging every space:
playgrounds,
    parking lots,
        and roads.

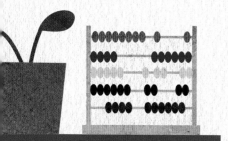

PARKING

U

As the water roils and rolls
it stirs up oil
and grime
and mud.
What a puddle-muddle

FLOOD!

Where do you suppose
all that mucky runoff goes?

It FLOWS . . .

into our waterways,
clogging rivers,
    ponds,
and lakes.

But, WAIT!

Can't we lessen all this mess?

YES!

Roll a barrel to a spout.
Catch the raindrops trickling out.
Watch them gather,
drop by drop.

Plink.

   Plip.

      Plop.

Water saved for droughty days.

Pitter-patter,

raindrops splatter
in the barrel
'til it fills,
then

S
 P
  I
   L
    L
     S.

Now what?

Make a trail of stones or bricks
or patchwork tiles
that winds and twists.
A path to ramble,
dance,
    and skip,
that shows the rain just where to go.

Where is that?

To a spongy, pooling place.
A saucer of land
to hold the rain
as it expands.

Not done yet . . .

Let's add some plants!

Lots of flowers,
grasses too.
Native ones with
tough, thick roots
that weave a net below the soil
to filter out that grime and oil
and guide the rain to . . .

PERCOLATE

deep
   deep
      down
into the ground.

OOOH, look at all those flowers bloom!

A rainbow bobbing
on the breeze
to welcome friends that
   hum
      buzz
         flutter
to a pollinator feast.

HEY . . .

in our garden,
we can spy
other wildlife stopping by!

Plink.

Plip.

Plop.

Now when raindrops drop,
we watch them patter,

splatter,

run

to the special place we've made
for the rain . . .

and everyone!

MAKE ROOM FOR RAIN

Follow these guidelines to create your own rain garden:

Choose a **downspout** from your roof, near where you plan to plant your garden.

Pick a spot at least ten feet from the building to plant your rain garden.

Make a **path** to lead the water from the downspout to the rain garden. You can form your path with a downspout extender, stones, or other materials.

Use a **rope and flags** to lay out the garden's boundary. Determine its size and depth based on the size of your roof and the amount of rain that will go into the garden.

Dig your rain garden into a **shallow bowl**. Make sure the bottom is flat and the sides are gently sloped. This will help hold the rain that spills from the path.

You can conduct a simple **infiltration test** to determine how much runoff your garden can absorb. Dig a hole about the size of a coffee can. Fill the hole with water and insert a ruler. Mark the starting water level on the ruler. Measure again after 1 hour.

Use this chart to figure out how deep to dig your rain garden. (If the change in water is less than ⅛ of an inch, the area is not suitable for a rain garden.)

Change in Water Level (inches)/ 1 hour	Rain Garden Depth (inches)
⅛–¼	3
¼–⅜	6
⅜–½	9
over ½	12

In places that receive enough rainfall, consider adding a **rain barrel** beneath one or more of the downspouts on your building. You can use the rain collected in the barrel to water your garden during dry spells.

Plant flowers and grasses. Visit a local nursery to find **native plants**: plants that grow naturally in your area. Choose flowers that bloom at different times so you will have a rainbow of colors all season.

Water the plants regularly when they are first planted. Native plants can survive drought when they are mature, but they need tender care when they are new.

Rain gardens provide **habitat** for hummingbirds, butterflies, bees, and other pollinators. These creatures move pollen between flowers so the plants can make seeds and reproduce.

Native plants grow deep **roots**, some as far as twenty feet down! Sturdy roots help the plants survive extreme conditions like droughts and floods. They also act as a sponge, soaking up stormwater runoff. The roots also filter pollution out of the water. Then bacteria in the soil work to break the pollution down. Your rain garden will help reduce the amount of storm water washed away to rivers and lakes.

You can make a difference, one drop of rain at a time!

Rainfall amount and soil type vary around the country, and so do the details of building a rain garden.

Many city and state environmental and water resource departments, college extension departments, and other organizations have information about rain gardening. Check with them for the best plan for your area.

Other resources include:

United States Environmental Protection Agency: www.epa.gov/soakuptherain/soak-rain-rain-gardens

Groundwater Foundation: groundwater.org/rain-gardens

Three Rivers Rain Garden Alliance: www.raingardenalliance.org

DO NOT DIG until you know where all of the utility lines are in your yard, so you don't accidentally hit them.